Top 10 Expired Objections

Know what words to say and when to say them.

William J. May

Dedication

To Gwen -
The love of my life, my true north, my backbone to
my success. With all my heart with all my love. Thank
you for always being there for me and always
reminding me, with the Lord's help, there's nothing
that I cannot accomplish. Thank you.

Get This Book as a Course

http://expiredlistingmastery101.com

Foreword

I first met William in a Real Estate group on Facebook. I remember seeing a post where he was making thousands of calls a week. At the time, I was lucky to hand dial 100 numbers a day.

I sent him over a message and set up a call with him to see what he was doing. From then on, we have been friends and talk regularly.

William is an expert in learning scripts, dialogues and objections! When he told me he was writing this book and asked if I would write a foreword, I told him I thought the idea for this book was excellent!

I think there should be more training material like this in the Real Estate industry.

Here is the best advice I can give you on learning to overcome objections when prospecting on the phone. The first thing many agents have to do is overcome the fear of getting on the phone. I really believe the best way for you to overcome the fear is to have a system that you can have confidence in and practice as much as possible.

Part of that system is learning to overcome objections and practicing those objections over and over. I believe it is one of the fundamentals of the business.

The fundamentals are the boring things you do over and over every day. They are also the skills you need to win every day.

If you take this book and the information in it, find a role play partner, and practice them over and over, I guarantee it will change your business. What I will do for you also is, help you find a roleplay partner today! All you need to do is join my Facebook Group: Real estate agents that REALLY work and post:

"I just bought William May's book and I need a role play Partner".

You will get one ASAP.

Jason Morris
Real Estate Agents that Really Work

P.S. I have a special gift I am going to give you. Actually, it is my #1 tool in my listing Tool Box. It is my Pre-listing package. Download it for free at: http://bit.ly/2v6hWwx

Introduction

Expired Listings, easy pickings, low hanging fruit, the number one source for successful Real Estate Agents to make a living, yeah, okay, I have heard it all. So, you're probably asking…

> "If this is the case, why aren't all Realtors jumping on the Expired Listing bandwagon since this is an easy source of business?"

The non-sugar-coated truth is…it's hard work! Trying to pull the Expired Listing from that low-hanging vine will, in most cases, break your damn back. If not your back, then your spirit. I've decided to put pen to paper or fingers to keyboard, and try to assist other Agents in working with Expired Listings.

When I first started in the business I was using thirty-year-old scripts. It seemed like the Expired Listings that I called knew what I was going to say, even before I said it. Not to mention, the Expired person was pissed off because I wasn't the only Agent calling them at 8 o'clock in the morning.

I don't know where you practice Real Estate, but I'm sure competition across the country is fierce. I practice in Los Angeles, California. It seems like everyone and their mother has a Real Estate license. Even though my market is flooded with Real Estate Agents, in my experience, most Agents do not work Expired Listings.

If you put forth the effort to pick up this book, that means you're looking for something to help your Real Estate business to succeed. Let's imagine this for a moment: you're working with Expired Listings and you're closing deals. You have the confidence of a top producer. Why? Because you *are* a Top Producer.

There's no Expired Listing under the sun, that you cannot sell. Everyone at the office is looking up to you. You and your family can just go on vacations whenever you want. You have the house you want, the car you want, and the lifestyle you want. You have made up your mind to succeed, and you know the only way to fail in this business is by giving up or quitting.

In the beginning of my Real Estate career, my biggest challenge working with Expired Listings was picking up the phone and knowing what to say. Every successful Real Estate Agent starts at zero, and with that uncertainty in the beginning.

Please do not let the title of this book fool you. Yes, I'll help you with the most common objections for Expireds. But also, this book is crammed with a lot of useful information that's designed to help fellow Agents across the country deal with the most common objections and a few tips that helped me along the way.

This will be my first book in **The Real Estate Agent Success Series**. It is written by an Agent that is actually in the trenches, closing deals, working with clients, and getting the job done.

There's so many coaches and programs on the Internet, you'll go broke purchasing them all. I was once a new Agent struggling for knowledge, scared of the business, unsure of myself, wondering what to do next. That's exactly why I took the time to write this book. To help other Agents to succeed and to reassure them it is possible to be successful in Real Estate without taking you to the bank.

I hope this book will help you in your business and help those Expired Listings to finally get sold with your help. I would say "good luck", but with a positive attitude, determination, and consistency, you won't need it.
Go get them!

Working with Expired Listings

Like I mentioned earlier, it's been said Expired Listings are easy pickings or low-hanging fruit, and they are the number one source of business for most successful Agents that are willing to work them.

That may be the case, but if you ever talk to Agents who have been in the business for a while and do not work Expired Listings, they have a lot to say about them and it is mostly negative.

Veteran Agent: "Well you know, Sonny, those Expired Listings...they're not realistic on price; they are difficult people. If they did want to sell, they would be sold already!"

It's definitely one way to look at it, but I look at it like this: please do not take offense, but just maybe it might be the Agent's fault. Of course, the Agent wanted to sell the property and have a successful closing for his clients. This is how he/she makes his/her money and can feed his/her family. Everyone must eat, right? Of course.

There's a lot of moving parts at play. Maybe the Agent couldn't handle the objections or the seller's unrealistic value of their property, so he/she listed the property too high. As a result, the property does not sell/expires. Perhaps the Agent didn't have a listing presentation strong enough to convey his/her professionalism that he/she knows what needs to be done to sell the property at the highest possible price.

It could have been a weak CMA or Competitive Market Analysis that did not show the proper market value of the property. Another big problem I see with Agents is that they are commission hungry. They are not presenting themselves as a Real Estate Professional. It could have been one, or mixture of all these things.

Frankly, your job as a Real Estate Professional is to demonstrate to your client that you're the man or woman for the job. These are the comps in the neighborhood, and the market is going to bare what the market is going to bare for the property. It is my job as your Real Estate Agent to get you the most money possible. For me to do that, we must work together so we can have a successful conclusion to the deal.

One thing I've learned from my wise and true broker:

"There's nothing wrong with a house that the right price won't fix."

For Expired Listings, prices are usually the number one reason why the property did not sell. Nine times out of ten, the seller wants way too much for their property. It's our job as professional Real Estate Agents to make sure that we demonstrate to our clients the best strategies to get their property sold without leading them into the Expired wasteland.

Expired Listing and Agent Mindset

Working with Expired Listings, you must have a certain kind of mindset. You also must understand your potential Expired client mindset as well.

Remember this, if you don't remember anything else:

"It's your own mindset that determines your success in Real Estate or not."

Expired Mindset

Depending on when you're going to interact with the Expired determines their mind set in most cases. It's always a good idea to be ready to work early in the morning. Be ready to start calling at 7:45 or 8 o'clock.

Believe me, it's always best to learn from someone else's mistakes. I was always under the impression that Expired Listings in Los Angeles were rude, crazy, or just outright insane people. If these people really wanted to sell, they would be sold by now. Absolutely something must be wrong with these people. "Of course, they're expired!" I said to myself.

The reason I had that impression is because by the time I got on the phones and started prospecting at 9,10, or 11 o'clock in the morning, they had already been contacted by so many other Agents that they were pissed off. **No wonder!** That's why they were cussing me out, hanging up in my face, not wanting to be bothered with me or anyone else that mentions Real Estate!

I can't tell you how many times I heard this from different trainers:

"You must be the first one in the morning to contact Expired Listings."

Agent Mindset

Playing the Expired prospecting game, you must be aware of your own mindset. Of course, we understand that the Expired Listing is going to be upset that their home did not sell. This might sound crazy, but this is a good thing. You may ask why is this a good thing? Motivation! The homeowner still wants to sell their home and move.
This is where you stick out your chest, raise your head up high, and speak with authority and confidence.

Your affirmation:

"I'm a Top Expired Listing Specialist and I help people! Who's next?"

Have the mindset that you are a Real Estate Professional. I can help this homeowner sell their home and net them more money than any other Agent.

I didn't realize it then, but I now know how important it is to be one of the first Agents or the first Agent to contact expired listings in the morning.

One week, I decided to start prospecting an hour earlier in the morning, so I started calling at 8 o'clock. I noticed right off the bat, for the first 30 minutes of my prospecting, that I started having actual conversations with Expireds. The rest is history.

From that morning on, I've been calling Expired Listings starting at 7:45 or 8 o'clock in the morning. I have a total mind shift when it comes to working with Expired Listings now. Understand I'm not saying just because I'm calling them earlier that it's easy pickings. No, it's still hard work, but I learned something very valuable that 90% of the Real Estate Agents don't know or don't realize:

From 7:45 to 8:30AM is probably the absolute best time to have a beneficial conversation with a new Expired Listing.

My strategy is:
1. Find out their motivation.
2. Get their information.
3. Set an appointment.
4. Follow up.

Very rarely does an Expired call become a list for me. You must have the mindset that you have to follow up with them consistently to develop a relationship. In this way, you build rapport, so you can close the business when it makes sense for them.

Do Not Ever Be Commission Hungry

A commission-hungry vulture of a Real Estate Agent: all he wants to do is close another sale at the client's expense. Clients can always smell this a mile away. You're a professional. You know what you're doing, and without you, they will not be able to walk away from the closing table with the most money possible.

If you understand where the Expired client mindset is coming from, you're already ahead of the game because you know they're going to be upset that their house didn't sell. They were unable to move on with their plans, and now they have a million and one Agents calling for their home driving them crazy. Your main goal is not to get the listing on the first contact. Your main goal is to see if you can help.

To help, you have to go through a good Expired script. In this way you can check their motivation and, in most cases, obtain useful information that you can use to help them make a decision that will best help their family. Through the conversation if it looks like you can help, you would want to set an appointment to meet or at least see the property. In this way you can at least have an opportunity to meet the potential client face-to-face.

There's nothing better than a belly-to-belly, face-to-face meeting in sales. I tell you there's nothing more uplifting than you helping people and getting paid for it.

Always remember:

"If you look out for their best interest, it will serve you well."

Frequently Asked Questions

Where do I get the numbers?

There's several different services to get Expired Listings or numbers in general. There's not as many landlines as there used to be. Just keep in mind, every year the lines get fewer and fewer.

I've tried several different Expired Listing services. In my opinion, you would have to try various services and see which service works best in your market.

A list of Expired Listing services in no particular order:

1. Red X
   http://www.theredx.com/expireds/
2. Landvoice.com
   https://landvoice.com/expireds/
3. Vulcan7.com
   https://www.vulcan7.com/
4. ReboGateway.com
   http://www.rebogateway.com/intro/home
5. MojoSells.com
   http://www.mojosells.com/ (I personally use and endorse)
6. EspressoAgent.com
   https://espressoagent.com/expireds/

If you would like to look some up yourself. Here are some sites I have used.

Bonus
Spokeo.com, Intelius.com, Dexknows.com

What is the best Expired training course?

If you check the Internet, you will probably see a quite few Expired Listing programs out there on the market. In my opinion, Borino Expired Plus (https://expiredplus.com/) is the best.

The reason why I feel his course is so beneficial to new and existing Real Estate Agents is because the creator learned in one of the hardest markets to be successful in: Southern California.

Also, his program is not just fluff, but hours and hours of continuous, relevant content that is updated constantly. If you don't believe me, check his YouTube Channel (https://www.youtube.com/channel/UCL5mptC7KYHmx10xWZXokng) or his Facebook Group: https://www.facebook.com/groups/rockstar.agents/. See how his students are kicking Real Estate A$$!

Like I mentioned before, there are tons of expired listing programs on the market. I know about quite a few, but I only suggest the ones I've tried personally.

I cannot stress this enough: I don't want new Agents or existing Agents to go through what I went through, getting robbed blind by so-called Real Estate gurus selling you on the latest silver bullet or new magic pill. If I've told you once, I've told you a thousand times, there's no silver bullet or magic pill to be successful in Real Estate. Only hard work, determination, and consistency will lead you to success in anything you do.

What is the best auto dialer to use?

You have Turbodial for Infusionsoft, Vulkan 7, Red Storm Dialer, and quite a few others. The whole purpose of using an auto-dialer is to be more efficient in your prospecting. There are many types of auto dialers. Some have a single line while others have a multi-line set up.

If you're a new Agent or just starting out calling Expired Listings, I would suggest you start with the old-fashioned method. Use your cell phone or office phone. These are high-quality leads. You do not want to lose the Expired Listing because of a bad or delayed connection.

When you're new at calling Expired Listings, it's best to get comfortable with calling them one at a time. Do not rush it. Take your time. If you work them in this way, your comfort level, and experience will increase. Only then would I suggest using an auto-dialer.

My auto-dialer of choice is the Mojo Sales Dialer. I can cold call/circle prospect with three lines at a time. The system can call through 300 numbers per hour. It is a tremendous time-saver over calling one at a time on your own phone. And for a bonus, if I don't have that many numbers to call, I can adjust the dialing system to two lines or even just one.

Another reason why I like Mojo: in their system you can set up groups. I have three groups for Expired Listings: New Expires, Prime Expires, and Old Expires.

New Expired

New Expired Listings are from zero to fourteen days. When I call through these listings, I will hand-dial these numbers or use the Mojo one-line dialer. This is more efficient than using the multi-line dialer on these leads.

Prime Expired

Prime Expired listings are from day fifteen to three months. When I call through the Prime Expired list, I use the two-line dialer. This group tends to have a few more numbers than the New Expireds group. I usually call this list several times because from day fourteen to three months is usually where you get the most Expired Listings or turn over. That means they probably will list with you if you have good follow-up. Sometimes, they have already listed with another Agent.

Old Expired

Old Expired Listings are 3 months old or older. I use the three-line dialer when I'm calling through the old Expireds. As you can imagine, I have a ton of old expired numbers in this group. If they do not relist or tell me to take them off my list, I will keep them in that Old Expired group.

If you don't use Mojo, you can still use this system or a variation of the system on any other dialer/database system.

What is the best CRM to use?

What is the best Customer Relationship Management System (CRM) to use? Well, the short and crazy answer is whatever CRM you're comfortable in using. There are so many programs out there, I'm not even going to begin to try to list them.

What I would suggest if you're a new Agent, and you've made up your mind on which expired system to use to retrieve your data, it's a pretty good bet that the expired system would be the best CRM system to start with. You're familiar with it, and you know how it works. That's the system you're going to be using daily.

If you're an Agent that's been in the game for a while and tired of your current CRM, experiment with different CRM's that are available. Usually they'll have a free trial or promotion to get your precious business.

Okay, okay, I'll name a few:

- Top Producer
  http://www.topproducer.com/products/top-producer-crm
- Red X
  http://www.theredx.com/
- MojoDialer
  http://www.mojosells.com/

- Infusionsoft
  https://www.infusionsoft.com/product/features/small-business-crm
- Salesforce
  https://www.salesforce.com/
- BoomTown
  https://boomtownroi.com/features/predictive-crm/

…and on and on and on. You get the picture.

Well William, what CRM do you use? I use two CRM's. Yes, I'm crazy like that. The truth is, for right now, it's best for me to use two CRM's in my business. Eventually, that may change. Like I mentioned earlier, you have to treat your business like a living, growing business. When it grows, you must grow with it.

I used the Mojo Dialer and Contactually. (http://try.contactually.com/)

I have to give Mojo credit in the last few years they have developed into a very powerful CRM with a three-line dialer. I'm not going to go into detail. I primarily use Mojo for the dialing system to circle prospect/cold calling, Expired, For Sale By Owners, and my People Farm.

Contactually is the second CRM that I use for the simple interface and the ease-of-use. I primarily use Contactually for working my Sphere of Influence (SOI) and my database. Unfortunately, Contactually doesn't have a dialing system, but I wouldn't hold that against them.

Just take your time. Do your own due diligence. See which program best fits you, your business, and your personality.

Should I leave a message?

Should I, or shouldn't I leave a message? That is the great debate amongst Real Estate Agents. I will tell you this: if you do not leave a message you're one hundred percent guaranteed not to receive a call back regarding your message.

In my experience when I first started cold-calling without a dialer, leaving messages took a lot of my time. However, I received two great listings from cold-calling and one I was able to double end. Leaving messages is like the lottery. You don't win unless you play!

As far as working with Expired Listings: if you have some experience calling them, you will notice after a few hours or days that the expired voicemail becomes full. For the first twenty-four to forty-eight hours the homeowner's phone is probably ringing off the hook. They're mad, upset, and frustrated. In some cases, they turn off or unplug the phone. An answering machine does all the work for them by screening the calls that come in.

Personally, I do not leave a message during the first few days. This is my decision. I know several Real Estate Agents that leave messages on the first and second call. Remember back in the beginning of this book when I talked about the Expired Mindset?

They're getting bombarded with calls and messages. Yes, I'm among the Agents who are calling the Expired Listing when it first hits my computer screen. I'm trying to reach the potential client, so I can help them out of their situation. When I'm calling through the numbers again after about a week or so, that's when I use the Mojo Dialer to drop a voicemail to the Expired Listing. By this time, the craziness has subsided somewhat, and they're not so angry or hostile. In most cases, they are more open to return an Agent's phone call.

How should I follow up with Expireds?
It basically depends on the Expired itself. Each one is different in their own way. Studies have shown that

Expired Listings usually relist within three weeks. If you're lucky enough to actually speak with them and they say they definitely need to sell their home, follow-up is mandatory!

I'm sure you've heard "money is in the follow-up"? There are several ways to follow up.

This is the down and dirty version:

1. **Make the first initial call.** If no answer, call two or three times a day for two weeks. In this way, you're cleaning your list from bad numbers, wrong numbers, and the Do-Not-Call List. At the end of the first week if you have not made contact, leave a message if possible. (Remember to rotate through your different phone numbers you call out on.)

2. **You made contact.** Congratulations! These contacts can fall in several different categories, but for this book, we're keeping it simple. Follow up. Remember the 80/20 rule. The majority the people you call or speak with are going to result in some sort of issue. Just understand, that's part of the business: the Game of Expireds. Shake it off, and move on. We have some money to make.

If you have a nice decent conversation, but they're not sure when they're going to relist, ask when is the best time to check back. Whatever they say, cut that in half. After you get off the phone, send a thank you card. Make mention of something about the conversation: the reason why they're moving, where they're going, or how you can help, etc.

Whatever database you're using, make sure you give them a call a week later to see if they got your card. What you're doing is building rapport. If you're able to get their email address, then send them your information that same day, and put them on a monthly email drip campaign with market stats or something else of value.

3. **The best way is always in person.** Have a mini resume (which I use from the Barino Expired Plus system) handy, or something of value that shows you're a professional and you have testimonials of satisfied clients. If you're new in the business and do not yet have past sales, speak with your broker about using the brokerage sales stats. When I was new in the business, I had to make do with what I had at the time. Remember, you always have to crawl before you can walk.

Where do I find good role play partners?

To be a master at your craft of communicating, role playing your scripts plays an essential part in developing your skills. You can lose tens of thousands of dollars on what you say or what you don't say.

Your communication skills are like a muscle. You must work it out every day, every week, and every month. At some point they'll be a part of you, ingrained in you. Your words will be who you are.

You might be one of those who say, "I don't like scripts, it doesn't sound right, it's not me."

Did you ever come to think that every time you pick up a phone and say "hello", that's a script? What is your favorite movie of all time? No matter what the answer is, I guarantee you the actors that played in that movie, all worked with scripts.

The best thing about scripts is that they're totally evolving. You'll learn the basic scripts, and you will build those basic scripts into more advanced scripts. As you practice and internalize these scripts, they become a part of you. This takes hours and hours of practicing, rehearsing, and real-world experience.

I would suggest that you find good role play partner in Jason Morris' Facebook Group: https://www.facebook.com/groups/RealEstateAgentsthatREALLYwork

At the time of this publication, the group is close to 20,000 members ready and willing to share information on prospecting, marketing, and role playing. It's not uncommon in the group to get multiple answers from Agents all around the country that are successful in Real Estate.

Is memorizing my scripts enough to be successful?

Knowing the script and dialogues is not enough. You need to adapt to the prospect the same way a boxer bobs and weaves during a fight not to get hit. Understand you have control over your destiny. As a matter of fact, you need to understand your action goals and your result goals. It's been said many times: Real Estate is a numbers game. Understanding your result goals and number goals will help you achieve this.

You might say a result goal is saying "I'm going to set up one appointment a day". That is something you don't have control over, but you do have control over your action goals.

Action goals might be something like making up your mind to have the discipline to prospect three hours a day; five days a week. You have control over your action goals. If you continue with the actions, it will build up like The Compound Effect. Once you start taking listings, you'll start generating momentum.

The more prospecting that you do, the better you will get with your communication (scripts and dialogues). The more interaction you have with your clients, the better you will become with your customer service. The more people you help, the more deals you will close.

Sometimes it's not what you say, or how you say it. Sometimes the hardest part is just picking up the phone and making that first call. I'm sure you understand now, an Agent that works Expired Listings understands there is a method to the madness.

Objections vs. Conditions

Objections vs. Conditions, what's the difference between the two? Well, it's simple, really.
Example of an Objection:
An Objection is basically an obstacle to overcome. Either the client needs more information on something, or does not trust you. They could just be trying to blow you off. Your job as a Real Estate Professional is to determine which one it is.

Let's say for example, a client asks you:

"How many homes have you sold in my area?"

In my opinion this is clearly a sign of no connection with the seller. You need to establish rapport or a connection with the seller to show them that you're a professional and that you sell homes. Not only that you sell homes, but you sell them faster, and for more money than your competition.

You must understand that, if the seller decides to use you, they are most likely putting the most expensive Real Estate asset they own in your hands. Don't be surprised if the seller is asking you qualifying questions until they feel comfortable and confident that they are making the right decision.

In this example, you can use your numbers, or if you're new, you can use your company's area sales. Always be familiar with your numbers and your company's numbers so this way you are always on top of your game.

Example:
Seller: How many homes have you sold in my area?

You: Mr. Seller, I'm happy to let you know, in the last 60 days WE have sold over thirty-eight properties. I'm not saying this to impress you, but to impress upon you, that out of thirty-eight closed sales, we have sold twenty-three of those properties over asking price. You would agree with me, this type of service would be beneficial to you and your family, correct?

After they say yes.... go for the close!

Example of a Close:
You: Mr. Seller, let's do this...my schedule books up quickly. Let's get something on the calendar. What works best for your schedule? Later this week, early afternoon, the evenings, or would the weekend be better for your schedule?

Tip: You will notice throughout this book. When it comes to handling objections. I repeat, affirm, and ask another question. When I'm giving examples, I try to have several different closes and several different responses. This way, you're not saying the same thing repeatedly sounding like a robot.

Example of a Condition:
A condition, on the other hand, is basically a bridge you cannot cross or a wall you cannot climb over. Conditions are an immediate roadblock when communicating with a client or a potential client.

Understand, just like an objection there are different kinds of conditions. Most will derail your plans immediately, but some can resolve over time.

For instance:
Seller: Yes, Mr. May, we're definitely going to sell our house but not until our son graduates from high school this coming June.

This is an immediate condition you cannot do anything about, but on the other hand, this is still a high-value lead. Stay in contact and offer them things of value. You should be able to convert them when the time is right.

Another example of the condition...
Seller: Yes, Mr. May, I would love to sell, but I just can't sell and pay off my tax lien and have money to move on with my life. The numbers do not work out.

This is another example of a condition. Unless the potential client comes up with the finances to pay off the tax lien or his property value rises enough for him to move forward, there's nothing you can do in this situation. In this situation, I would put the client in my People Farm and stay in touch. Maintaining and growing that relationship with follow-up will generate referrals for you in the future. **The money is in the follow-up!**

The sooner you identify an objection or condition, the sooner you know which direction to proceed with the lead. I can only give you an outline, definition, or my own experience. Always remember each market is different, so the best advice comes with your own experience.

Consistency

In every part of your Real Estate career you must have consistency, especially in your prospecting. You need to set a schedule everyday where you prospect, follow up, and go on appointments on a consistent basis. Your Real Estate career depends on it.

This may sound crazy or absurd, but you must think of your Real Estate career as a **Living Breathing Business** that you constantly have control over.

There is a saying in Real Estate:

"The leads you generate today will feed you and your family for three months, six months, and up to a year from now."

Think of your Real Estate career as a business, and your Real Estate business as a job. You are the star employee of your business. Since you are also the owner/operator of your successful Real Estate business, you have a business plan in place. You also have a set business schedule you follow each work week.

To do this on a successful, consistent basis, you must set up a schedule or routine and stick to it.

or example, let's say your schedule for prospecting is Monday through Friday 8AM to 11:30AM. This is the designated time for you to call all your prospects like new Expireds and old Expireds, FSBO, SOI, database, and follow-ups. You get the idea.

From 11:30 to 1PM you have your lunch and run errands.

From 1 o'clock to 6PM can be a mixture of things that could change daily. Regardless, you should be doing prospecting or lead-nurturing activities during this time such as:

- Follow-up
- Calling back Expireds or For Sale By Owners
- Working on your afternoon appointments

In my experience, setting listing appointments ranges between 2 o'clock or 5 o'clock in the afternoon. Very seldom am I taking listing appointments later than that. If you're a starving Realtor or you need to jumpstart your business again, take the listing at whatever time the client is available and willing to meet with you.

The Weekend
If you're a new Real Estate Agent or just need to jump start your business, work every single weekend

you can get your hands on. Weekends are the best days to generate business. Nine times out of ten, more people are home on the weekends than any other day of the week.

You can do Open Houses, door knocking, or phone prospecting. The best thing to do is to get face-to-face, belly-to-belly with as many potential customers as you can. Once you have a steady flow of income, then take the weekends off so you can spend more time with your family. That's priceless!

It's a Numbers Game!

One thing I love about Real Estate is that it's dependable and predictable. If you work hard enough and long enough, eventually you will succeed. The only way you will not succeed in Real Estate is if you give up, throw in the towel, or call it quits. In this business you must have consistency to win.

Real Estate is a game you can win. Do not let anyone tell you otherwise... even yourself. You made it this far, you can go all the way. Did you know the numbers are in your favor? Did you know that homeowners are **70% more likely to use the first Agent that they encounter?** Sounds like good news to me.

Before I go deep, I would like to tell you a quick story of the sower. Most likely you have probably heard of this story of a farmer who is planting seeds. One day, the farmer walks around his farm scattering seeds in different places.

One area of the farm where the seeds were scattered, the birds came quickly and ate the seeds. Some fell on the rocks with light soil and began to grow, but on the first hot day, they died off. Other seeds fell in the thorns and as the seeds began to grow, the thorns choked the life out of them. Some seeds fell on rich, good ground and produced a good crop for the farmer.

The purpose of this story is to explain that prospecting is a numbers game, or what you can call the law of averages. You might have even heard of the 80/20 rule. It all boils down to you knowing your numbers. Numbers don't lie.

Do you remember earlier in the book when I mentioned you have a living business in Real Estate? Knowing your numbers plays a huge role in having a successful business.

Let's talk numbers! When you call Expireds keep track of your numbers. This way, over time, you have a track record to review. Let's say for example, an experienced Expired Listing Specialist finds a listing after speaking to eighty people. On the other hand, an Agent with not so much experience working Expireds might take the listing after talking to 160 people or more. Let's go even deeper. A brand-new Agent might not even take a listing at all after talking to more than 300 Expired Listings.

You must put all the pieces together to have the numbers work in your favor. What do I mean by this?

Practice, practice, and more practice. Take the time every day to practice your scripts and dialogues.

You may not understand this, but this is an investment in your future. The more Expireds you talk to, the more comfortable you get with speaking to them, and the more you realize they all have the same objections.

When you start out, prospecting Expireds is going to be hard and daunting. Please understand this is a normal process. To become successful, you have to crawl before you can walk. You have to walk before you can run. It might take you two weeks, a month, or six months to become proficient in dealing with Expireds.

I want you to know you have several things in common with successful mega Agents. We all put our shoes on one foot at a time. At some point, we all started at zero. The cool thing about this whole process is it's only going to be difficult in the beginning, but once you start becoming used to the process, it will get easier and easier.

When you first start calling Expireds, you are going to realize a lot of people are going to be upset, angry, and frustrated. That's only normal when they listed the house with an Agent that didn't get the job done for whatever reason. That derailed their plans. Of course, you would be upset too if you wanted to move and weren't able to. If you understand their mindset, you are more likely to be able to not take their frustration personally. It's part of the Real Estate game like I said before.

I don't understand how a lot of these coaches and trainers throw out these ridiculous numbers like, "for every ten Expireds you call, you get one listing," or something ridiculous like that. I believe in real-world numbers and it's not pretty. It's not meant to be. Being successful, like I said, is hard work.

These numbers are just an example of the worst-case scenario. As you know, your results may vary. Once you start the process and get more familiar with your prospecting style and contact ratio, the numbers will develop a pattern that you can use to build your business for success.

Let's say you have to dial 100 numbers to get two contacts.

Let's say you need 100 contacts to generate two good leads.

Let's say you need fifty leads to generate one appointment.

Finally, let's say you take three appointments to get one listing.

As you look at these numbers, that might get you a little nervous, but it gives you an idea on how to manage your business based on what you need to do. As you prospect Expireds, get more familiar with them, and follow up with them, your numbers will improve. Your confidence will increase, your conversions will start taking off, you'll start taking more listings, and closing transactions because you embraced working with the numbers.

The farmer had to manage his crop the same way you have to manage your prospects. When you call an Expired and they're not ready, now you have to nurture that prospect, stay in front of them, send them things of value, and answer their questions. Of course, you're going to lose most of the time: they're going to tell you not call them anymore or that they're on the Do-Not-Call list.

You might have a good conversation with them since you built a little rapport. However, like some of the seeds that fell on the stony ground, next time you look up, they listed with another Agent. It will happen to you. It happens to the best of us.

With the select few that you stay in consistent contact and follow up with, they will come to understand your UVP (Unique Value Proposition). They will value your service and list their home with you. After the smoke clears and the dust settles, you will have a successful closing with a satisfied client for life. Priceless!

Tools of the Trade

Your Calendar

Whether it's a physical calendar or digital calendar, your calendar is one of the main tools for being successful in Real Estate. Become accustomed to scheduling everything in your calendar. Spending time with the family, your family vacations, anything and everything must go into the calendar, so you can stay on track with your business.

Make sure you schedule your prospecting as a recurring appointment. Do not schedule your listing appointments during prospecting hours. The only exception to the rule is, if you're new or you're in a sales slump, then of course drop everything and get that listing!

The end game is to make your business grow and to make money. Once you start taking listings, you will start closing listings. You will start generating momentum. Once that occurs, you will start doing what top Agents do: schedule their appointments away from prospecting hours. Soon enough, you will see yourself as a top-producing Agent.

Workstation

You need a quiet, distraction-free work environment. This could be your work office, home office, or just a quiet room with no distractions. If you have a designated workstation such as your office, the main thing you need to do before you start prospecting is turn off all social media, email, TV, and put your cell phone on airplane mode if you're not using it. Oh yes, do not forget to put the do-not-disturb sign on your door knob.

Computer or Laptop

In this tech-savvy world, I don't see how it's even possible to have a Real Estate business without a computer. The computer or laptop doesn't have to be state-of-the-art, and have all the bells and whistles known to man as long as you have a digital device that will help you prospect. I mainly work from my home PC. At the office, I use my laptop. It's very mobile and convenient when I have to pick up and go to a conference room or to a meeting in another Agent's office.

I also use an iPad on the go. This is very convenient for me for several reasons. I could use it in a meeting or at a business lunch. I can conduct general prospecting on-the-go where I can log into my Mojo dialing system or into my CRM. Also, I take it with me on listing presentations just in case I need to show them any detail on comparable sales in the area.

Telephone

You must have a good, reliable cell phone. I would suggest a smartphone.
Don't hold it against me, but I am an Android type of guy. I do know of other successful Agents who use Apple phones as well.

Whatever brand you choose, make sure that you have a dependable service provider. It doesn't make sense for you to have a $1,000 phone that you can't use to make a ten-cent phone call or not have a good Internet connection. It's just not worth it.

Your Car

Your automobile is probably the most valuable piece of prospecting equipment that you will ever own. You can call, email, snail mail, text, or send smoke signals. Whatever form of prospecting you decide to do, there is nothing more valuable than being face-to-face, belly-to-belly with a potential client.

If you take the time to survey Expired Listings like I have done, you will see this time and time again if you ask them.

You: Mr./Mrs. Seller, the three weeks your home has been off the market, how many phone calls have you received from Agents?

Seller: Thousands.

You: Besides myself, how many Agents have come to your door?

Seller: Just you.

As you can see, you don't have to be a rocket scientist or a genius to figure out all you must do.

Do what other Agents are not willing or too lazy to do to be successful in Real Estate.

Let me be the first to warn you: when you pull up to your first Expired Listing, the hardest part is getting out of the car. Once you make contact, you'll see the fear that you built up in your head was just unnecessary drama.

You will be asking yourself: why wasn't I doing this sooner?

Rules of Engagement

Are you ready to get down and dirty with expired objection handling?

Great, let me explain a few things to you. There's no magic bullet. There's no magic words or miraculous script that will make clients fall at your feet and beg you to sign the listing agreement. Even if you were born the silver-tongued devil himself, there's no way to convince someone to sell a high-ticket item such as a single-family residence without motivation.

Yeah, you could probably convince someone to buy a candy bar that your kid is selling from school. I can guarantee you this, there's no way you can persuade somebody to buy a house or to sell their house when they don't want to. Don't even try.

Most Agents don't understand we're not here just to collect a paycheck. We are here to service our clients. That primarily includes moving mountains, jumping over roadblocks, and God only knows what else. So basically, our job is making the Real Estate transaction as seamless as possible, so they can move forward with their lives.

We are problem solvers. If they're looking to move up, move down, or go sideways, we're here to solve whatever problems they may have. We are here to help them sell their house for the most money possible.

Do not let your client expire in the first place

This goes without saying. Maybe I should say it just so you know that whatever you do, try your best not to have your client's property expire. In most cases when a property expires, the Agent has done a disservice to their clients.

I know every time a property expires, it's not the Agent's fault. As Real Estate Professionals, it's our job to educate our clients and have them understand that we are the professional, and the information that we're providing will get their home sold in the shortest amount of time with the most money in their pocket.

I have found there are several ways to connect with expired sellers, or anyone for that matter, using different systems. NLP is one of them. NLP stands for Neuro-Linguistic Programming. If you talk to different Real Estate Agents, they have their own take on NLP. Once you get the basics down, it will help you connect and interact with your clients on a deeper emotional level.

Another system I like to use are the DISC profiles. DISC profiles consist of four key traits which are:

1. Dominance
2. Influencing
3. Steadiness
4. Compliance

When it comes to selling Real Estate, these traits must be learned in order to communicate with people in ways they will best respond to you. I suggest you go online and take a DISC assessment test for yourself.

Education is always key. If you want to be successful in Real Estate, you have to upgrade your education. Take the time to learn NLP and the DISC profile system. In doing this, you will become more knowledgeable and more successful than the average Real Estate Agent.

Consistency

We talked about this in an earlier chapter. Always be consistent in everything you do in your Real Estate business.

Never, never, never argue with a potential client!

I learned a long time ago always agree, agree, agree, and agree. Even if you disagree, you better agree! Some people just want to start an argument, and it's funny to me when they try to argue with me and I agree with them. They're stumped.

Let me clarify, this doesn't mean I'm agreeing to whatever they are saying. I *validate and agree* with them and move on with the conversation. You must realize that some people are stuck on stupid, or have just made up their minds on what they believe. When you run across a person like this, you have to make an educated decision about when is the best time to just move on.

I could tell you this, but you must learn from your own experience. Working with difficult people is not worth it. Believe me when I tell you that you want to work with people who know you, like you, and trust you rather than someone that doesn't believe you're worth what you charge. These types of people will not accept your professional opinion regarding their property, and just don't have faith in your proven system to get their home sold for the most amount of money.

In the beginning of my Real Estate career, I was working with my Pastor from childhood. He knew me quite well. He also knew I was new in the business. I guess because he was in the military, he was used to getting his way. There were quite a few times we bumped heads. I learned a lot from that experience. I was always professional when he brought up my inexperience in the business and how he sold properties before.

I informed him that after the great foreclosure crisis, a lot of things had changed. Even though I may not have had the experience as a veteran Real Estate Agent, I studied very hard and passed my Real Estate exam on the first try. The State of California Department of Real Estate issued me my salesman's license soon after. With the help of the number one brokerage, two top brokers, and 150 Agents at my office, I have more than enough experience to fall back on if I need it to sell your property for top dollar.

It came to the point where I had to tell him I cared about our friendship so much that I was willing to sacrifice our business relationship so that we could remain friends. I told him that he had my permission to find a Real Estate Agent that was a better fit for him and his needs. There were no hard feelings, and to this day, we're still friends.

In the beginning of my career, I was kind of slow with firing difficult and crazy people. But now if I feel that I cannot help them, and we do not see eye-to-eye, I let them go quick, fast, and in a hurry. In my Real Estate career, I've had many coaches and trainers.

Bob Loeffler taught me this:

**It's not my job
To make crazy people sane,
Stupid people smart,
Mean people nice.
It's my job to find…
Nice, Sane, Smart People…
That I can help, and do business with.**

As I look back on that experience, I did not know anything about NLP or the DISC profiles. Who knows what would have happened if I knew then what I know now.

There's another saying in Real Estate:

"Some of your best listings are the ones you don't take."

What is your (UVP) Unique Value Proposition?

Seller: What is my unique value proposition? Or Why should I hire you?
You: Well, I specialize in selling expired homes other Agents were not able to sell. I'm like a Real Estate doctor. I examine the Expired Listing, how was it was listed, pictures, description, everything.

Step two, I communicate with the seller, check their motivation to see if they're realistic on price, see if I would be comfortable working with them, preview their property, and see if their property is in sellable condition in relation to the sale price.

Once I have all the information and review all the facts regarding the property, I will give them a plan of action on how we can sell their house, make the home show-ready, and available to potential buyers. I will have the property cleaned and staged, update the MLS with current information, professional photos, and a detailed description of the property and the neighborhood including the city to draw in buyers.

In most cases, you will price the home at a lower price. This is not always the case, but most of the time, that is the reason the home expired in the first place. It's our job as professional Real Estate Agents not to be involved in Real Estate malpractice by not having the strength of will or the professionalism to be honest with the seller regarding price.

Demonstrate to the seller that you can do more than put a sign in the yard that's a different color, and that you have a proven system to get their Expired Listing sold. This is your unique UVP!

Top 10 Objections

There is a method to the madness. No matter what script you decide to use, your goal is the same:

Generate appointments. Determine if this lead is worth following up, or if the lead is trash.

Always repeat, affirm, and ask another question. Mirror and match the client. Let the potential client speak 80% of the time, and you, 20% of the time. The majority of your 20% should be asking questions. Statistics have shown the more someone talks, the more rapport you build. Focus on their needs and wants while keeping the end game in mind.

Top 10 Objections:

1. You're the fifteenth Agent to call me today!
2. Where were you when my house was on the market?
3. Do you have a buyer for my house?
4. We're going to list with the same Agent.
5. We're going to list with a new Agent.
6. We're going to take a break from the market and wait a while.
7. How are you different from my last Agent?

8. We changed our minds about selling/We're not selling!
9. What's your commission?
10. My last Agent said he'll cut his commission, will you?

1. You're the fifteenth Agent to call me today!

Response A
You: Wow… I'm the fifteenth Agent to give you a call this morning? Do you know what I have in common with those other Agents?
Seller: No. What?
You: They see the same thing I see: a beautiful home that should have sold! What do you think stopped your home from selling?

Response B
You: You don't say, fifteen Agents? Well, I can't speak for those other Agents, but your past Agent never informed me about your property. Let me ask you...how did you happen to pick your last Agent?

Response C
You: Wow, Mr. Seller, that's a lot of Agents to be calling you all at once. I don't know about you, but if it

was me, I'd be pissed off that my house did not sell, and now, all these Agents are calling me out of the blue. Mr. Seller, I know you are probably overwhelmed right now, but if you were able to get this home sold and move on with your plans, would you still want to do it?

2. Where were you when my house was on the market?

Golden Nugget:
This is the number one example why I say you should be one of the first ones to call the homeowner when their listing expires. If you're the first one to call them and they're upset because their previous Agent did not sell their home, that's usually a telltale sign that they have high motivation for selling and moving. If you wait until later that morning or that afternoon and you're the 500th Agent calling asking for the listing, it's safe to say they're pissed off because you're blowing up their phone. In their eyes, you're just like everyone else...a vulture Real Estate Agent trying to get the listing!

Response A
You: Working like a dog. Did you know, Mr./Mrs. Seller, while your property was on the market, we

sold over thrity-five homes. Let me ask Mr. Seller, I know your time is valuable. Were you just looking to list your property, or actually get your property sold?

Seller: Yes sold. (sample of a close I use)

You: Exactly, this is all I'm proposing. I would like to go over three things with you. First, I would like to pop by and show you exactly why your home did not sell. Second, I would like to show you a few things that will definitely draw in buyers interested in paying top dollar for your home. Mr. Seller, would you say that's pretty important?

Seller: Yes.

You: Finally, the third thing is I'm going to show you why my homes sell for top dollar. We can get together really quick today at 3PM or 5PM, or I have a 4PM and a 6:30PM tomorrow if that would be better for your schedule?

Response B

You: Working for my clients. An Agent's job is to generate the highest level of buyers to buy your home and get it sold. That was not the case for you. What will you expect from the next Agent you choose?

Response C

You: I can understand your frustration. You had your home on the mark for _____ months and only now the Agents come out of the woodwork. Let me ask, if you can still get your price and get your home sold in thirty to forty-five days would you still sell it?

3. Do you have a buyer for my house?

Response A
You: You know what, that's a good question. I don't know. I haven't seen your house yet. Are you still interested in selling?

Response B
You: I don't know. Our office has over fifty Agents that work with an average of three buyers each. If we can generate a full price offer and get you sold, that would definitely work for you and your family...right?

Response C
You: Let me ask, what type of buyer are you looking for? (No matter what they say...) Okay, we can agree the best buyer is someone that is ready and willing to pay your price, and can close escrow.

If I/we can generate that buyer and get you back on track with your original plans, are you ready to put us to work?

4. We're going to list with the same Agent.

Response A
You: I can understand that. So, you're going with the same Agent, is that correct?
Seller: Yes.
You: Okay let me ask you this, is fifteen or twenty minutes of your time worth possibly saving fifteen to twenty thousand of your equity?

Response B
You: I can understand that. Let me ask, what will your Agent do this time around to definitely get your home sold?

Response C
You: I can understand stand that, you were on the market for over a half a year. I don't know about you, but to me, that's a long time. If I can show you a proven plan that I use to sell homes for top dollar, would you like to hear more about it?

Response D
You: What can you possibly lose by spending fifteen to twenty minutes with me?

Response E

You: What can you possibly lose by getting a second opinion on your   most valuable asset?

Response F
You: What can you possibly lose by getting a second opinion with a powerful Agent such as myself. You do want to get the most money for your home, right?

Response G
You: What's most important to you in an Agent?

Response H
You: What is it about that other Agent that makes you want to stay with them?

Response I
You: What's more important to you, getting your home sold for top dollar with a powerful Agent, or doing a good friend a favor?

Response J
You: I can understand that. Are you familiar with the techniques we use to sell homes that other Agents were not able to get sold?

5. We're going to list with a new Agent.

Response A

You: Hey that's great! Have you already signed the contract with this Agent?

Seller: Yes.

You: Thank you for your time have a great day! (Example of a condition.)

Response B

You: Hey that's great! Have you already signed the contract with the other Agent?

Seller: Not yet.

You: OK, that sounds good. I would love to show you how I work. When would be the best time to show you?

Response C

You: Great, I would love to apply for the job. Are you familiar with the system I use to get my clients homes sold faster and for more money than other Agents?

Seller: No.

You: That's exactly why we should get together. I found it's best for my clients to meet in the afternoon or evenings. Would 4PM work or would 6PM be better for your schedule?

6. We're going to take a break from the market/We're going to wait.

Response A
You: I can understand that. How long will you be taking a break?
(Whatever they say, ask if you can keep in touch from time to time. If they say yes, ask for their e-mail.)
You: Mr./Mrs. Seller, what's your email so I can send you information about myself and how I work.

Response B
You: That makes sense. Your home was on the market for a minute. I feel your pain. What do you feel caused your home not to sell?

Response C
You: I can understand you want a break from the market. In the time your home was on the market, there were thirty-five homes that sold. If I was able to show you how our system can sell your home for top dollar, would you want to hear more about it?

Response D
You: Mr./Mrs. Seller, are you still interested in selling at some point?
Seller: Yes, at some point.

You: This is all I'm proposing: before you decide to keep it off the market and possibly cost yourself tens of thousands of dollars, let me pop by and show you how I work differently than your last Agent. The meeting should only take fifteen to twenty minutes to show you my proven system to get your property sold within ninety days. I'm available today at 2PM or 5PM, or would tomorrow at 3PM or 6PM work for you?

7. How are you different from my last Agent?

Response A
You: What I am hearing you say is, how will I sell your home when your last Agent couldn't get the job done. Is this correct?
Seller: Yes.
You: It's a detailed process. I would like to pop by in the afternoon or evening to show you. Would 5PM or 6PM work best for you and your family.

Response B
You: Well, I am glad you asked. My office and I actually get homes **sold.** In the last 6 months while your home was on the market we **sold over 125 homes.** Would that be different?

Seller: Yes.

You: Do you want to know the good news, Mr./Mrs. Seller?

Seller: Yes.

You: We can do the same for you and your family. Wouldn't that be great?

Response C

You: You would like to know how I am different from your last Agent, I can understand that. You probably heard telling is not selling. So, with your home's help, I can show you exactly why I'm different. This is all I'm proposing.

When we can find the time to meet, I would like to go over three things with you:
First, I would like to pop by and show you exactly why your home did not sell. Second, I want to show you a few things that will draw in qualified buyers interested in paying top dollar for your home. Mr. Seller, would you say that's pretty important for your bottom line?

Seller: Yes.

You: And the third thing is, I'm going to show you why my homes sell, and other Agents' homes do not sell in this marketplace. We can get together today at 5PM or would 6:30 tomorrow be better for your schedule?

8. We changed our minds about selling/we're not selling!

Response A
You: You changed your mind about selling because you couldn't get it sold, or because you're just frustrated with the process?
Seller: "The agent wasn't able to get our home sold." -OR- "Yes, we're just sick of having it on the marketing."
You: Mr./Mrs. Seller, I completely understand. Some of the finest homes don't sell the first time. Before you make up your mind and keep your property off the market for any length of time, let me pop by to see your home. This way, I can quickly diagnose your home, and tell you exactly why your home did not sell. I can also show you some proven techniques that we use to get similar homes like yours sold in your area. What would be the best time to show you? Today at 5PM or would 6:30 be better?

Response B
You: You changed your mind about selling, I can understand that. I'm just curious, at one point, you did want to sell...what changed?

Response C

You: I can understand where you are coming from. Selling or not selling is a business decision for you and your family. I'm just curious...if you can maximize the money that you could put in your pocket in the next thirty to forty-five days would you want to hear more about it?

9. What's your commission?

Tip: Never ever talk about commission before the appointment. If you do, you will shoot yourself in the foot and regret it. Trust me, I know!

Response A
You: That's a great question. In the state of California (or your state), the commission is negotiable. That will be the first thing we will talk about when I see you.

Response B
You: Well it's free, and what I mean by that is, I don't charge you a dime unless I/we get your home sold for the price and the terms you agree to.

Response C
You: I'm willing to work for whatever we can agree to. That will depend on a few things, such as current

market conditions, condition of the property, how much you want for the property, and how long you give me to sell it. I'm sure when we meet you'll be amazed on how I do business.

Response D
You: Mr./Mrs. Seller that's a great question. What I'm hearing you say is, you're really concerned about what you're going to net at the closing table. Am I right?

Response E
You: Mr./Mrs. Seller that will be the first thing we talk about when I see you. Our main goal is to use a proven system that will attract buyers who will pay top dollar for your home. Your goal is to make the most money for your home, isn't that right?

Response F
You: I can definitely understand your situation. I have several commission structures. Let's find a time when we can get together and work out the numbers, so we can see if it will make sense for you and your family. I'm sure like most of my clients, you're not going to move forward unless the numbers make sense.

10. My last Agent said he'll cut his commission, will you?

These answers are for when you're at the appointment. If you sent them a pre-list package with a net sheet, you will not have to go through these objections. They will already know how much you charge.

Response A
You: I can understand that. Your last Agent cut his commission, is that right?
Seller: Yes.
You: How did that work out for you?
Seller: Not good.
You: I definitely understand...everyone wants a deal. As you can see, cutting corners on the most expensive asset that you own is not financially productive, correct?
Seller: Yes.
You: So, let's do this: list your property at a standard 6% commission. That way, we can have all the buyer's Agents working extra hard to help us get your home sold at top dollar. Makes sense, right?

Response B
You: Mr./Mrs. Seller, your last Agent cut his commission I see. Do you realize when an Agent cuts

his commission, that affects your bottom line? Would you like to know why?

Seller: Sure.

You: Real estate is a commission-based business. In my opinion, this is extremely unethical. Did you know if an Agent looks at your listing in the MLS and see it is offering a discounted commission, that most Agents go right past it straight to your neighbor's home? You know, your competition down the street? So, let's do this: list your property at standard 6% commission. That way, we can get your property sold before your next neighbor closes escrow. Fair enough?

Response C

You: Your last Agent cut his commission, and you would like me to do the same correct?

Seller: Yes.

You: Usually a seller's home is their most valuable asset. Is this the case for you?

Seller: Yes.

You: I can understand that, and my job is to safeguard your equity and get you the most amount of money at the close of escrow, correct?

Seller: Yes.

You: So, let me ask you this quick question: if you were on an operating table about to have heart surgery, would you feel comfortable asking the doctor to give you a discount on the operation?

Seller: No.

You: So, if a Real Estate Professional is willing to discount his commission just to receive your business, how would you know for sure he's doing his/her very best to safeguard your financial equity you worked so hard to build up?

Seller: Well, I don't know.

You: So, you won't have any doubts, let's list your property at standard 6% commission. Then you'll know that I'm doing everything I can to safeguard your equity and get your home sold for top dollar.

Response D

You: I see, your last Agent cut his commission and you would like me to do the same. Is that right?

Seller: Yes.

You: My Real Estate experience has taught me that if I did discount my commission, it is the equivalent of malpractice in the medical industry. I'll be doing you a grave disservice. No, I will not cut my commission. Any other questions?

Summary

Congratulations! For taking the steps necessary to complete this book. I'm proud of you. Not everyone can work Expired Listings successfully. In reading this book, you now understand it takes more than just learning scripts or objection handlers to be successful. You must have a thick skin, brass balls, the courage, and the strength the push through when needed.

Like we discussed earlier There's a lot of moving parts at play: the Agent and Expired mindset. Knowing that part of the job when you're calling Expireds is understanding the emotional turmoil they're going through,
you're like a doctor interviewing a patient to see exactly what's going on. As their professional, it's up to you to prescribe the right course of treatment.

Unfortunately, we can't help everyone, no matter what you say, or what script you use. You have come to realize by reading this book that it's a numbers game. It's going to be hard, difficult, and sometimes confusing.

You will push on and push through the difficulties. One day soon, you will have your aha moment, and you will see a veil has been removed in front of you.

You will repeat your affirmation out loud every morning:

"I'm a Top Expired Listing Specialist and I help people! Who's next?"
"I'm a Top Expired Listing Specialist and I help people! Who's next?"

Now you can see your dreams turn into reality, the smell of success, and the feeling of victory. With all the hard work, determination, and focus, you now see yourself as a **Top Producer.**

My Way of Saying Thank You

I would like to say thank you for spending your hard-earned money purchasing this book, and most of all, for taking the time to learn the material inside it. We all need help from time to time, so I've included a few gifts for you.

Here are links to all of my courses. This is over 3 hours of content for less than $10 each. This is my way of saying "Thank You"!

Expired Listing Mastery 101
http://williejmayenterprises.com/thankyou101

New Real Estate Agent Business Plan
http://williejmayenterprises.com/bizplan

Open House Master Class for Real Estate Agents
http://williejmayenterprises.com/openhouse

Real Estate Agent Pre-List Package
http://williejmayenterprises.com/prelistpackage

Jason Morris
Jason is the creator of the Facebook Group:
https://www.facebook.com/groups/RealEstateAgentsthatREALLYwork

Don't forget to download his Pre-Listing Package for FREE - http://williejmayenterprises.com/Jasonsfreeprelistingpackage

About the Author

 William J. May is a successful Real Estate Agent in Southern California with several years under his belt. With the success of his YouTube channel, he has received tons of questions regarding his prospecting. He decided to take the time to write this book: *Top 10 Expired Objections* to help new and aspiring Agents to succeed. *Top 10 Expired Objections* is one of a series of books in **The Real Estate Agent Success Series** he is currently working on.

Made in the USA
Columbia, SC
16 March 2019